THE PORTAGE POETRY
SERIES

Series Titles

Everything Waits
Jonathan Graham

We Are Reckless
Christy Prahl

Always a Body
Molly Fuller

Bowed As If Laden With Snow
Megan Wildhood

Silent Letter
Gail Hanlon

New Wilderness
Jenifer DeBellis

Fulgurite
Catherine Kyle

The Body Is Burden and Delight
Sharon White

Bone Country
Linda Nemec Foster

Not Just the Fire
R.B. Simon

Monarch
Heather Bourbeau

The Walk to Cefalù
Lynne Viti

The Found Object Imagines a Life: New and Selected Poems
Mary Catherine Harper

Naming the Ghost
Emily Hockaday

Mourning
Dokubo Melford Goodhead

Messengers of the Gods: New and Selected Poems
Kathryn Gahl

After the 8-Ball
Colleen Alles

Careful Cartography
Devon Bohm

Broken On the Wheel
Barbara Costas-Biggs

Sparks and Disperses
Cathleen Cohen

Holding My Selves Together: New and Selected Poems
Margaret Rozga

Lost and Found Departments
Heather Dubrow

Marginal Notes
Alfonso Brezmes

The Almost-Children
Cassondra Windwalker

Meditations of a Beast
Kristine Ong Muslim

Praise for
Everything Waits

"In his majestic debut, Jonathan Graham's poems are deftly crafted and immensely curious about the world and the worlds inside the speaker. His attentiveness to the natural world is staggering: the imagery is so precise, so vivid it's like stepping into a landscape painting. Family and love and death are not subject matter, but other landscapes to navigate, to bring skin-close. There's no tension between the outer and inner. The beauty of the natural world charges the speaker, and the speaker's emotions alter the world. Graham has written a book rich with grace and music."

—Eduardo C. Corral
author of *Slow Lightning and Guillotine: Poems*

"These stunning poems make us ask if there really is this much grace in the world. Could there be, when lurking just behind all the beauty of the Ohio Valley lies pollution and death and the sudden whipsaw of life reminding us nothing is permanent—not even the transcendence we ride in these poems. Jonathan Graham is an American voice we need—right now, in this time. We've been waiting for this poet since James Wright. The deft image. The presence of place. Grace among the ruins. From the farm, to Wales, to church, to train tunnels with boys, these poems are the truth of life lived, life saved, life lost in front of us. This book captures what you thought language couldn't."

—Jeff Knorr
Sacramento City College
Sacramento Poet Laureate, Emeritus

"In this intimate collection of lyric poems, Graham unfolds a radiant tapestry woven of his life. Graham, who grew up in a tiny coal-mining town in Ohio and who ultimately left it, never has forgotten his tender connections to the natural world, his lost community of immigrant miners, his childhood, nor his beloveds. Despite the losses that mount all the way to the recent pandemic, the poems together offer a love story. Survival, resilience, and ultimately, a quietly joyful wisdom shape the arc of these beautifully made, compelling poems."

—Carol D Guerrero-Murphy
author of *Bright Path Dark River*

"The well of joy and sorrow within Jon Graham's poetry runs deep, offering us a perspective shaped by his three decades practicing emergency medicine. The poems reflect, too, on Jon's boyhood along the Ohio River, nestled in a small enclave of Czech coalminers, where he lived, laughed, and wept along with his community under the shadow of mountains of coal that both gave and took life from his own family and loved ones. Throughout *Everything Waits*, Jon Graham's fresh voice explores old and new worlds, starting in Appalachia and moving outward and onward. These poems lay bare his years, ones spent defying life's cave-ins, refusing to wallow, soaring upward."

—James B. De Monte
author of *Where Are Your People From?* and *Brotherhood*

"Jon Graham sings into being an intimate kinship with the hilly woodlands of his East Central Ohio. These poems are eloquent testaments to his widening circles of compassion for the living creatures and beauty around him. The boundaries of Graham's self are porous, as he embraces the life that inhabits his farm through the soft zone of his skin. 'From droplets on leaves / to air / into breath, / I can feel the thready pulse of prayer in the sky,' Graham writes. Thankfully, we can all step into the sanctuary of his poems and feel our selves softened and enlarged."

—David Hassler
Director, Wick Poetry Center
Kent State University

Everything Waits

poems

Jonathan Graham

Cornerstone Press
Stevens Point, Wisconsin

Cornerstone Press, Stevens Point, Wisconsin 54481
Copyright © 2023 Jonathan Graham
www.uwsp.edu/cornerstone

Printed in the United States of America by
Point Print and Design Studio, Stevens Point, Wisconsin

Library of Congress Control Number: 2023938192
ISBN: 978-1-960329-03-5

Cornerstone Press titles are produced in courses and internships offered by the
Department of English at the University of Wisconsin–Stevens Point.

DIRECTOR & PUBLISHER   EXECUTIVE EDITOR
Dr. Ross K. Tangedal   Jeff Snowbarger

SENIOR EDITORS
Lexie Neeley, Monica Swinick, Kala Buttke

PRESS STAFF
Carolyn Czerwinski, Zoie Dinehart, Kirsten Faulkner, Brett Hill, Julia Kaufman,
Maggie Payson, Cat Scheinost, Maria Scherer, Arianna Soto, Chloe Verhelst

for Martha McClay Graham
and her Lone Willow Gardens of the Sun

CONTENTS

Light Into Darkness

DARKNESS INTO LIGHT

I opened my eyes and saw the dark in all its original color.

—James Dickey

LIGHT INTO DARKNESS

Bending the Long Arc of Starlight

Sacred: our woods and orchards, meadows wide and windy with green
        leaning before the ground, the way sea waves
        slowly break and pool over sand.

In long grass, the shrump . . . shrump of walking, then boots pulled off
        at the door drop to earth's floor
        with the thud of a tree-fallen apple: gravity.

One untethered day I sit on the porch,
        boots off, and wait for the eclipse, feel the wild color

of white asters bend on the path down to the creek, move invisibly toward
        the sun, drop petals, fossil bones into silt

as if happening for eons. If I listen to the path, I hear wind's breath
        between the hills, and see someone barefoot

walk by, as if born right around here, or somewhere close, or that
        The Creator is from here,

                or at least stayed here once, if only
for an artisan's overnight, toying with relativity: Einstein's gravity bending

                the long arc of starlight around the eclipsing sun
as it nudges moon's dark shadow over the planet,
                heaven and earth each a turn with the light.

The Mane of a Horse

Everything waits.

A swayback Percheron tests the air,
leans his head into fence to ponder fields.
Today, he can no longer pull the hay wagon.
        Unshod feet drag him down into tall grass.

      Wind swirls his scraggly mane
as if he has already turned to grass,
as if he is already a part of the field,
        was from the very beginning
when his mother gave him to the land.

She comes back to him now in darkness,
leaves the beauty of her propriety inside him,
knows what to keep and what not to keep;
and the stars light the way for him,
        shine down their seeing
        and unseeing of things
        in front of him
        as if he was and is
        a part of an existence,
        a beyond no one understands.

Perhaps the mane of a horse is holy.
Still, the land goes on unimpeded.
Buzzards gather.
        Wings fold to bodies
        like hands in prayer.

Thrill of the Tunnel

Like a young teen's fascination with smoking his first stolen cigarette, the train tunnel from childhood looms in memory: distorted, a crooked picture plastered on a mountain of rock with tracks hanging off. In this dark opening, cut through veins of coal and sandstone at the base of a mountain, are four manholes, two on each side, carved into a wall only four feet away from the tracks. The holes are to be used if someone is in the tunnel when a train comes through.

I see four boys kneel to ground, fix their ears to tracks to listen: a locomotive can be detected a mile away. Once alerted, the boys run into the tunnel, fill the manholes, listen up close, first to the warning whistle then to the roar of the train, to see sparks fly, to feel the heavy, violent jolting as wheels strike joints between long rails of steel.

They feel the earth shake. The train passes at full speed only four feet away in the tunnel. Intense pressure in their ears gives them the same nirvana that follows witnessing violent death, in this case potentially their own. They do it for kicks, just for the thrill, to see if a new initiate pisses himself out of fear of being sucked out of the shallow manhole by the force of the train and dies in the tunnel.

Afterwards, the boys sit outside the tunnel on the trestle, fish for mud suckers in Wheeling Creek, drink hard cider and smoke cigarettes stolen from their fathers' secret stashes. I hear them laugh, carry on in the warm sunlight of an April Sunday afternoon. I hear them talk about the train, how they could have touched it by merely reaching out a hand if not paralyzed by fright. The boys are in the sweet time of their lives, before they are the ones who work in the mines, fill railroad cars with the black cargo trains carry to burn in mills downriver, making the Ohio Valley choke, stagger onto its face, fall and piss itself into a permanent, polluted sleep.

Ordinary Is the Color of March in Ohio

Ordinary. Grassy meadow, board fence, brambly brush, leafless trees,
  muddy lake, sky.
Everything gray-brown. I open the door from my room to the porch,
  the knob clicks as it turns.
On the hillside, one by one, twenty deer jerk their heads up to identify
  themselves, stare at me.
After a full half-minute, they bound all at once from the open meadow
  into brush,
their tails a flock of white doves, wings sailing low around the curve
  of hill.

I feel guilty for interrupting their solitude, sad the deer are gone
  from view.
Staring into the now empty field, my eyes dissect the gray-brown color
  of hillside to uncover a different day,
a day like today; instead of deer, a herd of brown cattle grazes
  in the field with two bulls in a shoving match.
Their heads massive, pitted against one another, each pushing
  with such force
the hill seems to tilt and spring back, tilt and spring back. This heaving
  and renewing continues until their hooves
churn up enough sod to reveal something dark underneath, more rich
  than ordinary soil, almost alive – black blood.
They strain and grunt until the younger bull, the one with less conviction,
  is pushed backwards uphill, where he snaps like matchsticks
four rungs of oak-board pasture fence. I see the pupils of his eyes dilate.
  He falls.

I'm not sure why I think of the bulls, unless it's their ordinary color,
  similar to the ordinary deer, hillside and lake,
the ordinary sky. I gaze across the valley into the open forest
  of leafless trees.
I see into the lay of the land, the trails, rocky craigs, low places where
  the deer now lie out of the wind away from drab-colored coyotes.
Everything so ordinary, all gray brown, the color of fighting bulls
  and deer running.

Though the deer are gone behind the hill, their image flashes, the color
    of them running
crosses the meadow as one body without realizing or even wanting
    to think about it.

Their ordinariness is the color of a spirit running, gathering all
    the gray-brown of this world inside it.
When I look hard, my eyes uncover white patches of long bones
    scattered in the hillside brush.

The Fawn

A bump of brown is suddenly there, with spots

that float on air like some unsettled mercy.

In the dimness of high grass and rising fog,

close to the big hind wheel

of the rolling tractor, a fawn hides.

Noise from the cutting bar and rotating wheel

of the shaking hay machine make her stand.

The tractor groans. I hit the cold brakes.

My first thought – where is this newborn's mother?

The fawn quivers, alone and wet with amnic dew.

Eyes of trees that line the meadow stare

down at her. The tractor fumes exhaust

into the lifting fog around us. Neither she

nor I have time to contemplate.

The fawn moves her head toward me,

then turns her eyes to the haybine – and,

after only a few first steps on earth, jumps,

injects herself into the cutting

teeth and thrashing wheel.

There isn't time to make it stop.

Walking Into Dawn

Blips on the screen of grass. Whimpers of trees.
Only the wind.

A blip again.
I hear another dewdrop fall,
or is it a heartbeat?
We are that close to touching.

Footsteps kick in the underbrush.
Whatever it is – more than one.
More than one.
A clutch of hatchling quail springs up.
Something billowy will be needed to hold them all.

First light –
the numinous flower of morning opens,
remembers its promise
to lead us into day.

From droplets on leaves
to air
into breath,
I can feel the thready pulse of prayer in the sky.

Diminutive Bird

In the oldest mountains
light at dawn shines slanted
above treetops in forests of evergreen, hardwood.
Creek riffles sparkle. Islands of tree leaves,
needles of pine shimmer.

Within the mountain treetops, hidden in the Black Hills
overlooking an irenic lake and this green meadow
watered by the first skiff of fallen snow,
at daybreak, a diminutive bird,
nearly extinct, appears.

Her singularity riles me to ponder
which law of being was violated
and what anthropogenic genius
fished out the gene pool.

Powder of fine marl, crystals of schist awaken to earth warming.
Old dust whorls across shadows of rock ledges, pillars of smooth stone.
Dew drips from leaves rich with tannin. Eyes fill with natural glory.
Feathery ears cock, listen for a cry of the heart – alive, close.

With coming light, the diminutive bird
hears the sound that draws the wounded
from the world. Below her on earth's floor,
bisphenol A leaches from droppings
into roots of trees.

Sitting in the Same Dark

I depended on Vera being there, in her kitchen,
   alone in the dark, time still left in the day,

waiting for it to end. I'd rattle the loose, round
   doorknob, our secret handshake, and hear:

Janka, that you? I'd answer: *Baba, I can't see you.*
   You there? She'd laugh.

I'd come in to her darkness, her saving of electric
   left over from Great Depression days.

There'd be a little light from the dial of the low-
   playing, plug-in radio, Vera's shadow

cast on the wall behind it, her form as straight-
   backed as the chair she sat in, both shadows

on the wall beside the table, it too, up against the wall.
   I'd take my seat in the empty chair

on the other side of the table and face out, the two
   of us sitting together, facing out.

What you doing sitting here in the dark? She'd tell me
   she was reading

the book she had in her mind, the one about the old country.
   She'd tell me the story time-after-time

about how she left at nineteen, hid in ditches of Ukraine
   with other young Slovaks and Jews by day,

then by night traveled to Odesa on the Black Sea
   in the same dark she sat in now.

I'd ask: *who were you hiding from in the ditches?*
  She'd say: *the soldiers*, then turn the pages

of her book with her breath. In the dark, I came to understand
  about the soldiers and ditches.

They became to me what they were to her, as the night took us in,
  then let us both go.

This Light of Home

The road home sometimes drifts to a place off-grid
    where quince and forsythia line cinder paths,

a green hand pump draws well water, horsehair
    in plastered paper covers walls, an outhouse

stands in lilacs; where a furnace in a hand-dug basement
    burns coal, and smoke settles over the pines.

A place where mason jars of golden peaches
    with rugged red centers age in an earthen cellar.

A bed covered in goose down, pillows of feather tick
    clouds. A washboard leans on a steel tub.

From a high window, white curtains billow in sunshine.
    Come nightfall, the book on a table. A candle

dances shadows on the wall: the flicker
    of a fragile pulse of light.

Springhouse

A shady wooded spot down the way from wild strawberries,
a diminutive house of weathered boards and sandstone,
        A-framed roof and hinged door:

Vera's sacred spring:
        home to a small striped snake
stretched along the cool flat of stone where a frog might sit
to watch a spotted salamander crawl to the bottom
        of this diamond-clear pool.
Sometimes, we keep a glass jar of concord grape juice
        there to cool.

        A silken place I love,
like opening the door to a dream of Pirene,
clean and secret in an unassuming ground crevice.
        Our voices lighten to whispers
when we come close, so not to disturb Pegasus drinking.

After filling our shiny smooth buckets, neither of us wants
        to let go our handhold with sanctity.
We share a dipper for the long walk home from this place
        where water springs from an aquifer.
A limestone cloud hides beneath the Appalachian earth
        in a nook so quiet and still
no one dares disrupt the spell of kindness it casts,
        except to drink.

End of the Road

Pulling all that was left from before and promises for what would be,
heavy-footed oxen and iron-rimmed-wheeled wagons

long ago crushed gray cinder and sandstone on Zane's Trace.
Now a byroad, the trail wanders

through the weary coal town of Midway.
After crossing the shallows

of a wide Ohio creek, the road furrows in mud, climbs uphill
from the bottomland,

meanders past a strategic springhouse welcome to both livestock
and pioneer, then rests

at the Stone House Inn, brown and thick like an overcoat
on a blustery day.

In the afterimage of the moving light they follow,
a brimming trough of water

awaits travelers at the entry. Fresh water, shady cool and dripping
wet from lathered horses' mouths,

is as treasured today as it was in those early days
of settling America. Pioneers filled dry wooden barrels,

carried only enough on their Conestoga wagons to get them over
the horizon to the end of the road

where it falls from one world into the next.

Lullaby to the Carroll Hills

She leans in close to my ear with her lips, hand cupped
    to concentrate her breath,
and whispers a lullaby to the land.

> *I can't keep myself away from her.*
> *I can't stop myself from listening*

to the lullaby. Swaying with the wagon, its slow-going journey
    rocks the yawning trees of sleep,
hypnotizes wind, tickles leaves, sends shivers down the spine
    of land, raises goosebumps on a grassy knoll.
The song plays over and over, warbles from the mule-drawn
    wagon as it rolls on the land, mellow and fertile.

The lullaby sings to pastures, ridgetops, to pastoral nooks
    where common folk
work and play away from malls, interstates. I watch them
    cut wood for winter fires,
tend to lambs and calves, till their soil. At last
    the song settles back
to the wagon, onto the lips of the woman with opiate hair,
    muse of woodland.
As my hand falls into hers, she leans in closer to my ear
    with her lips. Our pulses join.
The sky blushes. The Carroll Hills turn back to look, promise
    not to tell what happens next –
the day intertwining in air between us, until the world
    tilts, as if
earth has turned her head to look. The wagon halts, feels
    the deep rhythmic pulse
of a fracking well lurking on its pad hidden in trees:

> chirr   chirr   chirr

Slowly, air untwines. My muse, Calliope, utters
    a disbelieving sigh.
The great plates below us slip from deep within the land.
    The well retrieves liquid flesh

from the depths of the world where dinosaurs once roamed
    in bogs of peat until the sun fell out of the sky.
This murk of darkness from underneath muffles the lullaby,
    while from above,
leaves fall all at once from wilting branches of trees.

Elise Lester Is Gone

The night you died in your sleep of carbon
monoxide poisoning from a faulty furnace,

I was awakened by the force of my heart
pounding the inside wall of my chest,

shaking my body, the bed I was lying on,
the home I had rebuilt, the world I lived in.

My heart rapped fiercely, wanted
to warn you to turn off the heater, wanted

to wake you, cradle you as we once
held on to each other in my father's car

parked in the deserted alley,
sharing a first kiss and life's first passion.

Back then you were just a girl and me a boy.
We had our song "Angel Baby" that we

danced to when we met and played over
and over, not wanting a last kiss to ever come.

All the love songs ever written added up
cannot describe the wonder of that first love.

All the love poems in the world added up
could never say it right. How is it possible

to convince anyone, let alone myself, that half
the love we had for each other is gone?

A Silhouetted Blur of Wingspan Lives Within Me

Son, I wouldn't fault you if you burned your draft letter.
I'd go to Canada or join the Navy if I were you.
Like most folks, I just don't believe in the Vietnam War.

— _____, decorated
WWII Veteran
1968

I

Going fast. Real fast. No traffic in either direction, I turn the lights out,
    my borrowed '65 Stingray whining

on Ohio Route 62's straightaway
    through lowlands between Alliance and Salem, Youngstown.

From window and mirror, road ahead and behind glazed in moonlight,
    I look long enough to see in the dark, then hold my breath.

    No luggage. Traveling alone. Top down in summer wind, night
dangles above me, breathes down its careless precision of stars.

    The allure of night's needle in its vein draws me in.
Wind blows me sideways, moves me forward
    like a large bird breaking branches,

    spreading wings to create a small hole in the canopy and escape
the low-lying swamp-woods.

II

A silhouetted blur of wingspan lives within me: a frightened large bird,
    rising and painted into the moonglow of my mind.

The wingspan lifts above swamp-woods beside the road,
    hovers over treetops in the night.

From the speeding Stingray,
      I watch the wingspan soar into moonlight.

      Once in the foolish sky, I wonder why
the moonlit need to do it, why the indifference, the lights-out wish,

the willingness to give everything away,
      before my wingspan has its chance to touch the other side

      of night's world –
eclipse the shadow of everywhere and nowhere at once.

Still lost yet unafraid, I breathe again. My eyes open wide to catch
      the sprawl of a wave

from the distant white light of oncoming traffic, rivulets of napalm
      running from the dark jungle oceans away,

and I know how much I love the earth, the night air, and turn
      my headlights back on.

Contiguous Blue

for Woodstock and Vietnam

The world didn't ask for blue, but it came
in napalm, body counts, in words of songs for love,
peace in the beat of rock
to the blue crowd at White Lake,
water of two wings, where Jimi's white guitar
played redwhite&blue psychedelic, electrifying hills
in grassy New York fields.

A tall man read blue words from a notice –
it burned like a flag in the wind.

The one of our two turned beautifully blue,
then vanished sublime into shadow.

The other, called up by jungles in waves of oceans,
flew into blue, searched for beauty
where blue clouds moved like smoke
from the one
away to the other,
ever touching and ever touched by the sublime.

Beauty came.
Though the one would not see it,
the other found it there,
there in the far contiguous blue, a rain-star
the color of blue
that took the place of war.

Thunder in the Ears of Gods

In the dawn of Eos, our practice ordnance
delivered itself like unwanted mail
to the Live Impact Area
on the island of Vieques.

The real war was over.
We managed to climb out of it
and soar,
search for another universe,
a mirage of blue.
We suppressed ourselves
eagle high,
drank raindrops with Artemis
before they fell like holy water
from her glass,
touched the purest light of all,
delivered it to the so-called civilized world below.

Then we felt the long arms of Helios, her brother.
His hands held our canopy's face like a capsule in space
or a chalice at communion,
warmed the dust, floated it free
like sins forgiven,
suspended from the pull of gravitational misunderstanding.

Of course,
we radioed the clouds below,
pardoned them like crowds of ungrateful spectators
and warned that we,
the unwanted,
were passing through,

coming home,

lapping sound,

and to barricade the air
for the sonic boom to come.

Serene: The Way Smoke Found Its Way

Smoke filled the valley. Serene, the way it moved from madness of fire,
    curled around cats lingering in the yard for food, draped
    the empty pickup with melted headlights parked in the drive.

Smoke slithered into the most unlikely places, found long, veined
    yellow leaves of trees, violinists' fingers positioned on wiry branches
    at an outdoor symphony: all awaiting the wind's instruction to move.

But smoke needed no instruction. Slowly, as if surveying the scene of a crime
    or tragedy, it slunk around the burned foundation of log cabin
    as an ex-wife would look for answers to tell grown children,
    or discover the body of her former husband firemen couldn't find.

Smoke happened upon so many things: cigarette butts flipped nonchalantly
    into the shabby grass of the yard, skeletons of burned-up
    kerosene space heaters strewn in ash and rubble, no longer able
    to dump their disappointments into the air of the cabin.

Smoke wriggled into the cracked mirror of a lifetime of procrastination,
    piled high with broken woodwinds, brass horns bursting open the door
    of a nearby shanty, desperate for repair. For a moment, smoke imagined
    itself to be the breath of the music man, crawled into the mouthpiece
    of his favorite saxophone to play the one song he'd never before rehearsed,
    important now only because the tone of it might reveal something
    about what actually happened before the fire. But the only music it made
    was like the sound of wind passing through dark absent trees.

Smoke moved through the town into faces of people, even ones
    who had fled years before. It found its way into their eyes, then crept
    into their thoughts, made them wonder how this could happen,
    how a brother could perish like this, the same way his uncles and fathers
    of his neighbors did in the explosion at Willow Grove Mine. My brother,
    Joseph, was found beneath the collapsed timbers of a house he'd built, found
    just as the miners had been, though he had never entered a mine himself.

Smoke moved from the town's thoughts into its soul: serene,
    the way it found its way there – as if in a final quiet,
    as if it would never leave the comfort of silence,
    as if it belonged, there in that space empty of all but angels,
    so airy and free of guilt that smoke too easily slipped away
    into the missing heartbeat of the wind.

The Hum in the Wood

I

Cut in short pieces (easier to move from place to place, from time to time)
       by a Stihl saw that loved its work,
chunks of wood against a wooden fence leaned into the woodpile naturally:
old friends holding each other up.

This pile of wild-cherry wood was once a tall and thriving bee tree high on the hill
       overlooking our farmhouse
until last winter's blizzard took it down, scattered the bees once spring came.
       I discovered the tree
years ago quite by accident while repairing pasture fence.

The smell of honey in the hole first attracted me, drew me closer until
       I could hear the humming inside,
telling me of the honey factory and thousands of bee-wing vibrations within.
       Afterwards,
whenever farmwork took me to the hill, the tree always drew me back

to smell the honey, watch bees come and go, listen to the humming.
       Once it fell, the bees long gone
to another home, I could still hear the humming of the great tree lying
       on the ground.
Now, after cutting and stacking parts of it into a pile along the fence,
       I could yet hear
the tree or imagined I could, as though the woodpile had a heart
       and pulse of its own.

II

Still, the humming reminded me of the sound of another woodpile.
       Then, I had to order wood
for our fireplace as I had no land or trees of my own.
       The man who brought our wood
told me all too quickly and outright about his two young children, ages two
       and four, as if he were confessing a mortal sin.

As he stacked his wood in a pile against my fence, his hands moved nervously.
    Two winters ago
his children burned to death in a fire from a wood-burning stove
    whose chimney overheated.
The two children slept upstairs in a room directly above the stove, next to the chimney
    to better keep them warm in winter.
He said he could still hear the screams of the children.

His wife worked night shift as a nurse and was away. He was a volunteer fireman
    and went to the station
to be with his buddies when the call came in from a neighbor about the fire
    in his own home.
By the time he got to the house, it was too late.

After the fire, his wife left him. After he unloaded the truck, he reminded me
    to take care with the wood, and left me.
For days and days, I found myself gazing out the window at the woodpile stacked
    against the fence in my yard.

One cold, moonlit winter night, I was awakened by screaming. I wasn't certain if it
    came from the fire in the stove
or from the woodpile stacked in the cold shadow on snow in the yard,
    or if it was just a dream, a nightmare.
Regardless, I moved to another home, a farm where I could cut and stack
    my own wood.

I pile my own wood now, sometimes just imagining it to smell like honey, but mostly
    it has the fragrance of ordinary wood,
and I hear screams of children in a fire and check the wood for a pulse, and hum,
    and wail, and I weep with the cut-up wood,
lean it closer to the solid fence in my mind, which has become a woodpile
    stacked not only with its own short pieces of cut-up wood,
every one a story, but also with those others carried to me from their own faraway places
    and meant to be burned in other fires.

What We Were One Evening

From our star-bloom view in a red canoe, evening came
        as roses in the lakeside garden:

pendulant, tilted on the hill, as diaphanous as a long-dressed
        fragrance moving in gusts

with petals, and stems – thighs only wind could touch.
        My face,

my lips brushed the roses, a coloratura of garden song
        in theremin-stretched pink clouds

on horizon's last-light-of-day sky, moon-wound with pale
        melon-flowers,

delicate as quiet consolations. Soft slurps of lake water climbed
        the garden's grassy bank.

Tongues of clams licked dew dripping fresh from velvet folds
        of petals. We paddled our craft to shore,

the porch-lit house with its bee in the light at the screen door:
        Is. Is. Is –

what we were that evening – Roses. Roses. Roses. – areolar
        blossoms, warm and soft on summer's breasts.

We hid ourselves in shadows with fireflies, recluses
        outside time,

attracted, addicted to each other and the night like chocolate,
        or jouissance, or, of course the emotive roses,

looking up and up beyond the night's haze into *the blood*
        of the stars, desiring only our eyes.

Two Birds, a Wire, and a Complication

In the cold moment after we entered the parking lot,
wind swept over the wire above our heads,
and the wire hummed something warm inside.

Two doves appeared with the wind,
perched beside each other on the wire.
The birds looked down to us as we looked up to them:
mirror images from the street.

We recognized each other.
As we did, everything stopped, even the wind.

Clouds, puffed in the sky, became stationary like eyes.
Leaves turned, held their fleeting edge.
When our breath stilled,
we became fixed on the birds and the wire.

In that moment, in the whole world, only the doves moved.
Turning their heads to each other,
they leaned in slightly as if to touch,
but an invisible barrier like clear glass had built up between them.
Each bird loosened its grip on the wire,
then lifted a foot, walking its toes up the glass
until one's foot was directly opposite the other's,
as if they had joined.

If it weren't for the unforgiving complication of glass,
they would have touched and come together.
For the birds, this was union enough for today.

Then the day that had hidden in the time-frozen leaves of trees
walked back into the street to join us.

The wind went on with itself as it was,
swept the doves off the wire,
vaulted them into the sky,
swirled our faces as it moved down the street,
whisked us like leaves over stone
back into our parked car.

A Confession in Morning Rain,
a Woman in a Mirror, a Buzzard

Rain is coming before dawn the wind said.

As the movement of air on the dark hill behind the farmhouse brushed long grass
     like hair in a woman's mirror,
the first yes of the day came: fingers of rain before dawn finding something smooth
     as lips on fleshy fruit.

Leaves on the pear tree outside the window flinched to the touch of rain on the pear,
     as air from rain
tapped on the pane loud enough for a sound to be heard, a sigh. Awakened
     from sleep,
I could hear it up close. Yes, it was definitely from inside the room and not the rain,
     or was it?

As I equivocated, light came. A black buzzard landed on the slate roof of the barn
     outside the window.
It looked into the house, its eyes finding the woman in the mirror. So, I fingered
     the carrion eater away.
Rising from the rooftop, it spread its wings to fill the entire sky.

Then I knew we would be all right, the woman in the mirror and I, under the umbrella
     of the buzzard's wing.
The day would be good regardless, because light came through the spread feathers
     of the wing
to reveal the shadow of the bird in the mirror become smaller, smaller as it flew
     into the distance of time –
a silent confession disappearing in a crack in the sky like a dark blood spot
     on a white sheet slowly fading away.

The woman's fingers went on with what they would do. The naked hair hung down
     straight and relieved
near the interrupted white sheets of the bed. As lips of rain puckered the skin
     of the pear,
light stepped out of the air to murmur: yes, I understand in the cracked mirror
     of the buzzard's sky.

Rain is coming before dawn.

In the Sound of the Train: Your Sleeping Face

One night the stars will rearrange
into patterns I can understand.

One night the 4 AM whistle will blow,
the train turn itself back
from approaching fog along the river,
sparks of fire flying from tracks through night air
like the Perseids, showering.

One night fog will come and settle in the cottonwoods.
The river will recall this nearing daybreak,
promise to become less obscure.

This is the time of close breathing.

I remember the sound of your breath,
how the night air cooled around your face in repose,
how your breath would leap high above you for an instant
as if looking for someone who was never born.

I remember the softness of the down blanket,
the way it covered everything else,
everything that happened before,

so, when the first ray of light comes,
the dove leaves her roost outside the window,
air behind her wingbeats implodes,
leaving no trace of anything,
erasing everything that could have been wrong, or right,
or even dreamed of.

I hear the train again.
The sound shakes the earth and water in the river that runs away from it –
your sleeping face as intangible as what's left of a Perseid falling star,
only its vague reflection shines in the flowing river,
as if I would look for you there.

The Cold of Hiraeth: Poem for My Welsh Ancestors

That night, the earth ignored its spin, held back the pain
    from its tilt for a moment of consideration.
That night, the sky seemed far away, farther than it had ever
    been before,
as though removed from being a sky in the world
    I knew.
That night, wind blew from a place it had never blown
    from before,
a place different than I could ever have imagined it might
    originate, a place of longing.

That night, rain was a silent rain, a rain that didn't splatter
    on the roof
or drip from eaves – a rain that moved with wind, deep rain
    felt from within.
That night, I remember the cold, the kind of cold that queuing
    more wood for the fire wouldn't help,
a cold that might stay forever.

That night, I knew I wanted to go back home, knew I needed
    to go back,
but I'd forgotten the way, forgotten where it was, even forgotten
    what home was supposed to be.
That night, I felt I would never be able to find my way back.
    I couldn't even be certain I came from anywhere at all.

That night, I knew the only thing I could do, the only way
    I could understand,
was to walk out in the rain, close my eyes, lift my face
    to let Hiraeth run down my neck,
cover me with cold until the sky seemed not so far away,
    and the wind would understand,

and I could remember where I was from, the way back.
   I would go there
for a moment of consideration, recollect everything I ever
   knew or imagined.
All this was in the wind, the sky. No one else was there
   except the cold of the silent rain,
the cold of Hiraeth that let the sky close its eyes all around me
   and hold me still.

Communion Wine

Nic skryte sa nikdy nestrati.
(*Nothing hidden is ever lost.*)
—Luke 8:17

for my grandfather, Mike Troyanovich

Even my fingers are shaped like yours, they say. I grip
    the shovel
in the afterdamp that becomes more and more faint. I dig
    deeper into the mine tunnel:
still there is no light, no secret passage to air. For you
    the sky was always underground,

your breath laced with communion wine. One Sunday
    morning during Easter season, we stood
in front of Saint Nicholas Russian Orthodox Church
    in the Ohio coal town of Barton.
We had just confessed all our sins, received
    Holy Communion.
You hadn't drunk a drop in a year until the chalice
    of Father Kossi touched your lips
with communion wine. Your voice sounded unrepentant
    to your wife
when you announced in broken English: *Janka, peek me up*
    Duesday, ten 'clock nighttime, right cheer!

Then you walked into the neon lights of the hard-liners
    to begin your three-day binge.
You laid your paycheck on the bar, bought a round
    for the house
as if you'd never been away. An embittered somebody
    in our car
mumbled a choked-up whisper in Slovak: *nic skryte sa*
    nikdy nestrati
as we began the drive home, one person short, not dreaming
    that one day
it would all be written down, yet never assimilated.

As we rolled out of the church parking lot, grandchildren
    stared out the windows
at the fedora riding atop your swagger. My somebody
    grandmother squeezed her hands
more tightly around the steel-cold, crescendoed tremor
    of a lifetime of disdain.
We could feel her exhale the stale air from her lungs,
    listen to it cross the vibrating cords of her larynx,
stumble over her quivering lips. After she held her breath
    to steady herself,
she ejected the sour air of that under-her-breath utterance
    into our ears like an empty shell casing
from a pistol cartridge striking the cold floor, its bullet fired
    point blank into your swagger as:
you son of a bitch in English, plain as day.

Applewood, Butterflies, and Summer Rain

for Mike Troyanovich, my grandfather

I

Those first light rain-taps on a thin flat tin roof go
                                        pitapat . . . pitapat.
Ploppy-drops, tintinnabulations that make dust dance
before swimming away, warn goats who loathe
the splatter-sound of wetness and bleat to stay dry.

Wind swirls chaff from sweet hay off barn beams, while smoke
drifts scent of burning applewood from the yard.
A small fire, tended for cooking skewers of bacon, is dampened
                                        by drizzle.
A gray-whiskered grandfather and young boy run from rain
to shelter in the barn. A butterfly tags along.

II

In a sudden summer shower, a yellow swallowtail
paddles the current of air to an open door, asks to share dryness.
He lights on the back of my hand.

Shhh . . . Shhh – rainwater gushes from the downspout.
                        Summer whispers something out of sync.
Shhh . . . Shhh – someone is here.

The swallowtail pulses his wings slowly on the back of my hand
                                        to match heartbeats.
This soft joining of rhythms charms two lives: one from today,
one from before, and lifts a promise like a butterfly in smoke.
A memory rises above the talking sheets of falling water
as two people glisten – together again in summer rain.

   I think: *how is it possible to be with someone who is gone?*

But the butterfly and I persevere easily
until sunlight becomes serious again.
                              Wings dry to dust on my fingers.
I see the breadknife in the old man's hand cut a slice of rye
                              from a fresh-baked loaf.
I taste bacon dripping on rye: salt in the rain –

sating a wistful hunger.

The Cardinal's Broken Song

The broken song for the Willow Grove Mine Disaster
                    is forgotten until a tremor
shudders the ground. One clear morning each March,
                    at precisely the eleventh hour,
a reminder radiates from the 22 South tunnel. Something
                    trembles from below,
disturbs a cardinal. Momentarily off balance, his song
                    of solitary notes is broken
as he clutches a barren limb in a cold orchard
                    of bending apple trees
on the hill above Willow Grove.

The comfort of daybreak's cover of snow, a soft
                    understanding in slanted rays of sun
of a world purely golden only at this given hour
                    in winter light.
Shadows, still, of men in hard hats, colors encrypted in snow,
                    blend with moving shadows.
One pastel, a young woman, walks lively through the quiet
                    to a parked vehicle.
She feels something distant, pauses for the tremor.
                    Unaware of the tunnel
and for no good reason, she looks instinctively upward
                    through that ectoplasmic flash
from a fleeting trance to stare briefly into the golden light.

Then she straps her young son into his car seat almost identical
                    to her unmet uncle
cinching the safety buckle on his miner's belt. But before
                    she starts the engine to go,
looks upward once more from the shadows to the sky,
                    pausing without ever knowing why.
The cardinal regains his balance on the limb and resumes
                    his broken song.

Rolling on Red Dog

They toiled with picks and shovels in the darkness of Willow Grove, cutters digging coal from under the mountain. In obscurity with mine timbers, railroad cars, conveyor belts, boys became men and men grew old underground. They separated shale rock from bituminous coal, created tipplesful of black lumps loaded into railroad cars, leaving slag heaps of shale and coal dust that ignited and burned spontaneously for decades, smoldered into red dog gravel.

Carbide lights fixed to hardhats, metal lunch pails with names etched into lids swinging from hands covered with coal dust, miners broke out of tunnels at day's end, destined home to women barefoot on wooden floors of company row houses. Like slaves to the mine owners, they toiled together, lived the hard life, were paid in scrip to be redeemed only at the company store.

Money taken from miners' pay to cover funerals when they died kept their wives from suffering the cost. The coal companies didn't waste a thing, except maybe a human life or two, here and there, even spreading their red dog gravel on country roads to keep down mud and dust. They liked a clean operation.

When the explosion and cave-in occurred from bad air venting and buildup of methane at Willow Grove Mine in Southeastern Ohio's Belmont County, the coal companies brought out seventy-two caskets, filled the churches for the barefoot women. The hearses rolled on dustless red dog-covered roads up into the hills, closer to the sky: the airflow there spectacular. Names etched on stones paid for in advance.

A Stradivarius Sings in the Wood

As I walk through woods into snow,
swirls of white-star crystals surround me
like miniature moons circling a planet in the Milky Way.

One unusual snow-crystal, a tiny-windowed ice-capsule,
offers a look inside its wintry eye.
I see time there, light years of it yearning
for me to come inside, learn how things once were.

A violin appears. I wonder if I might be imagining I could play,
until I recall my mother Helena's Stradivarius dreams,
ones she had on winter days when light seemed old, impossible,
when she might wish for something unattainable.

Then the music of her beloved Mozart fills the air.
Allegro snowflakes spin around me in whole notes,
half notes, sharps and flats.
Oh, how she wishes I could play.

Deer come out of the woods stippled with snow,
their breath-crystals billowing frost.
They hear the Stradivarius play and move closer to the sound,
purity of music from three-hundred-year-old spruce
luthier, Antonio Stradivari, used to construct his violins.
As he once did, together we count the closeness of tree rings
in old trees from the Maunder Minimum.

Though the spruce, themselves, are gone, the deer and I now
are hypnotized by the Strad.
White-star crystals blanket our bodies.
Young trees in the wood around us bow with the weight of snow.
Even light years slow to listen to the violin sing,
as Helena's music falls to the ground, silver all around.

The Reverse of the Night I Was Dreaming In

Waiting for more stars to gather 'round like white stones
        arranged in a jumbled pattern,
the moon hung tangentially in the black sky, lingered
        up there on a lonely street corner.
The assemblage of stars held it all up, kept it from falling
        off sky's curb into the wobbly darkness.

From this very sky I pulled on a thread of string to find
        a long-ago kite
I'd left dangling by its tail from the top of a tall silver tree.
        Strange I should find it
in the dark like this. I remember flying it in the light
        of day in our backyard
while my mother nurtured her plot of zinnias and my brothers
        scrapped over a wiffleball game.

The place under the tree where my father parked his car
        was empty. Another tug on the string,
and the kite fell to the ground into that empty place.
        I went to it, discovered a ring of dark oil
in the pallid limestone, a black moon in a white sky:
        the reverse of the night I was dreaming in.

When my fingertip touched the dark spot, it felt thick
        like blood, warm and slick,
slipping away like something I couldn't remember:
        was it the Philadelphia Chromosome,
the genetic aberration linked to myeloid leukemia?

Oh yes, that was it, in the empty space where my father
        first taught me to fly a kite.
The story rests at an unusual angle in my mind, as if
        mathematically incongruent,
in a state of genetic improbability or denial, just as the moon
        was that night, hanging
tilted in the strange dark sky my mind had been living under.

DARKNESS INTO LIGHT

Cliff Swallows: Ars Poetica

for Maj Ragain, once greenvine to poets who read and sing
at Last Exit Books, Kent, Ohio.
(Maj passed after the third winter)

See the cliff wall at West Sister Island, Lake Erie,
    enisled where greenvine climbed rockface,
  marking the ideal place to build our nest
                    with mud, grass.

Hatching swallow clutches there, nestlings fledged,
    learned from us to twirl, trapeze the air,
  greenvine holding on nearby.

Two winters withstood, the nest three summers used.
    On the third winter, a harrowing came cold to land,
  froze ground and water hard, afflicted the root of greenvine,
             laid it down, unable to climb.

Thaw came. The cliff wall sweated out the cold
                   from itself,
    sweated out the nest, emptied it onto rocks
  far below, a last exit for nests cold
            still from surf.

Sun rose a radiance to land, stirring mud and grasses
    warm around the edge of the great lake's island melt
            of ice
  where the nest had been built. When we came back
            to it

after the third winter, hungry still to nest,
    we found our cliff wall
  had stood its ground and were neither

dissuaded nor surprised for loss of nest or downed greenvine.
    Though saddened, we had no sense of any failure.

We surveyed
        what had been left,

did for nesting that which needed to be done, alone,
     and took unthinkingly to wing and beak
    the task of rejoining mud and grass to rock
                in the shadow-mark of greenvine.

One River

They say they were once the same river.

They say that long ago, before sabertooth, even Nyasasaurus,
the earth's plates slipped and rose up, puckered where they rejoined like lips
of planet-sized jaws touching, then parted the prehistoric river
with the single sweep of a giant tectonic tongue.
One river's end sent north to Lake Erie,
the other south to the Muskingum and Ohio, on to the Mississippi.

You, Maj Ragain, were the first to tell me the story of our rivers
that day we met on my farm along the Tuscarawas at my daughter's wedding.

You said you, too, lived along a river, the Cuyahoga,
near the old Native American meeting place on the Standing Rock.

You contended the Cuyahoga and Tuscarawas were once the same river,
that since both you and I resided on the banks of this "same" river,
we were neighbors, brothers.

I believed you then as I believe you now in your poems.

A small fire flamed between us – a campfire,
kindling a relationship that included brotherhood
with the Cuyahoga and the Tuscarawas.

Even today, as we tend our common fire from different places:
me here, you not far, out a ways, down along the river –
we become the rivers and lie down in their thrum,
to reunite ahead, again as one river.

Beauty in the Echo of the Crooked River

After the reign of industry's irk and gall had ended,
    and time stared down from its hole in the sky,
        beauty came back to the crooked river,
    the river that first flows south then north to Lake Erie.
We reveled in the sound, its roar of whitewater
        in the glacial pass.
    Freedom
      held onto our senses
        as we shimmered on river current
          through the gorge,
      made a poem with wind, mist of morning
        rising with sun and heron from the jetty.

As the heron climbed
    above cottonwood and wild iris,
    a burden from our shoulders went with her,
      rode the avian call of the Cuyahoga
        echoing from the rocky ledges:

Cuyahoga   *Cuyahoga*   *Cuyahoga*

We eased our kayak into the slit of valley, swirled tight turns of boulders
      on past the Standing Rock,
  where a shady quiet place that owned the earth floated upon us.
  The dark shape of a whitetail
meandered tall green ribbons of grass and swaying trees, hither and yon,
    with the grace of a silhouette
      softly folding shadows, one atop the other.
      We stopped to rest, to drink the wind with her
        before the shooting rapids,
    and heard without listening
      the sound of each other breathing.

    Looking up from being down together,
we saw ruffled in the underside of the heron's sky
    our words form clouds gathering blue.

Rifle cracks from the urban ridgetop undid the spell,
        turned the heads of bird and deer
                away from the trance of wind and river,
        reminded us
                      that we were still here on earth.

The wild eye of our kayak,
            restless now,
                as the foreign sound moved dark closer,
      looked up to read the poem we made of the day,
        held it high like a fish, a solar kite,
                into the fading sun's golden yellow-fin light
                  before we put her back
                        to drop the edge,
                                fall,

fall into the light-bringer's gift of a campfire come for us
                      to stay right here the night,
      knowing we were the only imperfect
            in the perfect of the river,
                  the heron,
                    the wind.

Morning-After Campfire

A blue heron re-announces herself from shadows
where water once burned.
The crooked river runs the way the last glacier
directed it to run.

A glint of light shows the midnight glass of wine,
left standing at water's edge,
as still and bare as it was in the woman's hand.
Each thing like the other – interchangeable,
yet alone, not enough.

In dim silence, her warm sylphlike shape
stirs from the campfire,
then touches my spine, works its way
into my trembling body,
healing the imperfect loneliness within.

I watch it drift with the smoldering fire.

A gust of wind –
the heron, lighter than air, lifts above the river
into a sky that seems not to mind
having someone else inside it.

Something About Their Being There

In the White Mountains,
　　a loon listens for the echo of her wailing cry.
　　　　　　　　Wind's sail slackens,
　　　　　dies in The Balsams along the lakeshore.
　　　　　　　　　　At moonrise, a band of deer
　　　　　　　passes through Dixville Notch
　　into a grand hotel's valley of grassy dew.
　　　　　　A stillness folds shadows naked into nightfall.

In the open ballroom window's candlelight, fingers find strings,
　　a wrist guides a bow across waxed tautness.
　　　　　Music releases, comes pure, then ricochets
　　　　　　　over the lake's smoothness
　　　　　　　　　to fill the sky with violin stars.

At an overlook above the lake's far shore,
　　a pair of illusive silhouettes,
　　walking hand in hand with the moon behind them,
stops precipitously to listen to the sound of the violin. Something
　　　　　　　　about their being there
　　makes the candle flicker in the open window
　like an eye of starlight, the flickering
　　　　a sign of something unnamed, something greater
than the simple, erratic movement of a candle's flame,
　　　　　as if emotion, or expectation, or both
　　　　　　　have entered the eye of starlight –

and reflected onto the surface
　　of the deep pool of lake
　below the airy silhouettes –
　　　　that moment specters touch lips
　　　　　　in the echo of the loon's wailing cry.

Selection Is Everything

I

When the last drop of pure blue dripped like honey
      from the tip of the glacier,

its color brushed into the shadow where your hair
      touched your shoulder.

Then a silhouette of you was drawn, using only blue,
      with an intersectional curved line or two.

Imagination wondered whose breasted profile followed,
      sat next to you in the window

of the picture. Was it your genetically superimposed twin
      with a mind of her own, looking warily away,

hidden behind a necklace of neonic crystal in fragile balance
      and as voluptuous as blue ice?

II

Selection is everything – the way your face is turned away
      from light as if in pain,

knowing had the otherworldly artist's right brain
      tilted the brush

a fraction of a degree one way or the other, you would never
      have suffered, but been shaped into a rose

or the white gasp of a tree peony, lifted into the sky
      by a flight of drones

while apotheosizing bees licked drops of nectar ice blue
      from cloud-sized blooms

and made royal jelly
      right there on the pink of your lips.

Dune Walk After Our Vows

I

From the trailhead, a dozen walkways to the beach. Yet, our footprints met,
    mingled in the sand.
Destined, our toes etched nearly identical impressions, so close they touched
    and let us dream.
When we slept, the lull of a common surf rolled in our ears from the open sea,
    while sea oats marked our path through the dunes.

II

One morning, shivery wind whipped a grain of sand into the orb of a spider,
    a necklace across the bare shoulders of sea grass lining the path.
As you walked into it, the sand grain spun on your bosom in sunlight and wind,
    sparkled like a dune's diamond-gift.
The web draped across the curve of your body. The gift spun again, teetered
    in a way
no one could see it, or us, hidden from the world in the dunes.

III

Morning air swirled, kicked bits of sand into crevices of opposing, converging
    angles.
Sun warmed until wind, moving in slow motion, hefted our beach towel.
    Dunes tilted; heads lifted.
Eyes opened to the embryonic sky of the Isle of Palms.

IV

When we walked out of the dunes to the flatness that ran to the sea, surf-spray
    wind, pushing life over our skin, murmured: go faster, go faster.
Behind us, sand spumed seashells of light, and before us our footprints
    converged on the beach,
one inside the other – yours into mine, mine into yours, steps ahead
    of whatever might try to overtake us.

She Swims Unadorned

When the dolphin's back broke the surface of water, she painted
       moonlight in blue.
From the bridge over the intercoastal waterway, I saw the dive
       and bottlenose part underwater.
Plankton streamed from her sides as if a peacock spread an opalescent fan
       in a brackish water-garden.

The dolphin swam toward the arch beneath the bridge where I stood.
       As she came closer,
I felt a breeze touch my face as would the curved hand of someone
       I knew.
My eyes fixated on the underwater halo of light that spewed from the sides
       of the dolphin's nose.

Something about the way the light arced made me think of that night
       on Alexander Street in Charleston.
We were just married. The jazz of Bob James's piano bubbled luminescent
       from a cabinet.
A bottle of wine wobbled on the table, while pink curlicues of scampi
       dangled
on the edge of the grill smoking from our second story overlook.

We hadn't been with each other in a week, so it wasn't long before
       reflected light on the floor,
the walls, and ceiling of our antebellum flat curled, twisted
       in crazy nighttime directions.

I remembered how your back curved, your hair falling down over it
       as you knelt on the cypress floor,
leaned on the loblolly sill. I watched you look, unadorned,
       into the night lights of downtown Charleston
through the rose color swimming in the stemmed glass
       you held in your hand.

From the bridge, I watched the dolphin roll in water below me.
       When she broke the surface,
the curve of her back whispered something mad into the night.
       Then she dove,
slipped deep into the earth's avail, left me far behind, my eyes
       scouring for a glimmer, wave after receding wave.

Alaskan Waterfall in Spring

Spring – all things flow through a valley of green time.
        Wind and meltwater riffle
the Copper River. Swallowtail wings pulse our faces.
        Catching no sockeye for lunch,
I pull a red apple she packed (just in case) from the knapsack,
        then watch easily from boulders of granite
arranged naturally in shade under trees of an alpine garden.
        In sunlight before me, a freefall of water
anticipates its tumble from a rockface onto the unbridled half
        of our team. Cascades of hair hug her body.

I sit away, unobtrusive, under trees tall with branches that filter
        light from the sky.
Some of it is hers. Some mine. Some together ours.
        She smiles:
something to do with the apple we share. From the top
        of the mountain,
clouds in a circle cleansing the far, a great gush of water falls,
        bucketsful break all at once
to wet her skin silver. Magnified by the sun, she is more
        than flesh:
a glistening-spirit has entered the edge of her smile.

As she stands naked, drying in the light, our eye-twinkle
        in time glows more than any other,
happier than even the snow-capped peaks that stare
        across the wide Chugach Valley,
more daring than the brown bear, who, for a long sniff,
        concocted interest in our otherworldly scent.
The moment is more grace-filled than anything either of us
        has seen or touched,
will see or touch, until we hike in some faraway spring
        to interwind at the waterfall
and find everything again as it was – even in a place
        we've never been.

End of the String

Purple kite. String in a ball. Wind on the hills.
Red leaves blow: day stars in meadow grass.
 Sun sparkles. Everything open. Climbing.

Give it more string, she says! Give it more string!
 Feel the pull in your hands!

As the cord peels away, the kite flies higher, higher, purpling
 the air, ground-shadow disappears.

My children run, skip and cartwheel, surge ahead,
 dogs chase after.

They reach for their mother's hair, long in wind
 like prairie grass.

Dancing in a circle, they bark and scream: *let it go!*
 Let it go!

When I do, the sky takes in the kite, folds around it
 a wide circle.

 I see the string's end
pulled through clouds to the circle's center.

I hear voices, purpling. We chase the string in the sky,
 all of us running, pulled to the light.

 We shriek: *wait for me . . . wait for me*
as we reach, reach, reach for the end of the string,

then reel it back into a ball to carry home:
hopelessness and hope at once
 in their own small circle,

with the kite and its tail lifted, held above ground like a flag
trembling. String passed to hands of children. Hair long
 in the wind. Barking dogs lick and chase after.

The Kingfisher Sees Through Slow Rain

Slow rain falls into the last sorrows of snow.
Into cold mist, with a crest so perfect
as if he slipped out of a photograph in a bird book,
a big river kingfisher returns to the half-frozen lake,
lights on a willow branch,
counts on it to hold and hangs on.

If you gaze through his eyes into this slow rain, you learn
that kingfisher was first bird after dove to leave Noah's Ark:
orange sun at his breast, blue sky at his back.

You see what he saw then is different from what he sees now:
a warmer thaw, new life's twitch earth-nervous
as it skims the lake's surface, watery again,
filled with hungry minnows, springtime-trembly.

A Soft Depression in Snow

A soft depression
stained red.
No tracks
led to or fro,
so sky
seems likely:
made the stain
of blood
on snow.

No trace left
of a struggle:
no fur
or feather,
no imprint
of talon
or impression
of flailed wing
or tail.
Only
red on white
in the soft depression.

Fear was here
before me,
and lay
paralytic
in this spot,
this soft depression
in the silence
of snow:
pale,
breathless,
unable
to tell me
anything more.

Boy with Sand in his Eyes

For the boy in the sand, there was no air. His sister, sitting only feet away,
    in the air, became a ballerina; his brother a musician,
but he, covered in sand and having no air, became in this world only
    what he was thus far: a child.

Actually, it wasn't that simple. There was drama. After his father dumped
    the load of playground sand
from the truck onto the driveway, there were screams from the other children.
    His mother ran
from inside their home, dove into sand with her hands then disappeared.
    The father shoveled,
shoveled sand until sweat poured from his face onto his hands.

A neighbor called first responders. When they uncovered the boy, he had sand
    in his eyes. Petechiae covered his face and neck.
Efforts at resuscitation began immediately. They rushed him to the hospital.
    There was never a pulse,
but he was so young, only four, weightless and ethereal, that I tried
    to revive him, revive him for the rest of my life.

His mother was with him at the bedside; one hand held by the chaplain,
    the other wiping sand from the boy's face.
When I finally stopped, before the room would be left to itself again,
    I saw the circular clock on the wall
kick back on, its hands begin to move, time going on as before
    what never should have happened,
or that maybe didn't really happen, maybe was just imagination gone
    berserk, beyond all possibility.

Then I saw the mother's eyes as she held the hands of the ballerina
    and the musician.
I saw their eyes and knew it was real, that the boy with sand in his eyes
    was gone.
I called home to ask about my own four-year-old son, and when
    I removed the surgical gloves from my hands,
the powder turned to sand. Everything stopped, as if a small hand
    reached out to turn an hourglass:
the world reset itself to begin all over again.

She Bloomed Back Into the World

The gurney crashed down the corridor, surrounded
        by triage nurses.
Like a small swarm of bees on summer's last flower, the nurses
        bagged a blue morning glory:
a young woman, with one tattooed arm flailing to the side,
        dripped fresh blood
from a needle track to the floor. I trailed as if the track
        was music
played by a Pied Piper of blood, the refrain I'd heard over and over
        in my life.

As I followed, I wondered if we'd used all our Narcan.
        She was the seventh overdose
of the weekend: a vile batch of heroin from the streets
        of Dayton.
Actually, heroin laced with carfentanyl, that illicit monster
        opioid ten-thousand times more potent.

The woman wasn't breathing, pupils pinpoint, needle tracks
        on both arms, ankles, groin,
even one over the jugular on her neck, but my fingers found a pulse –
        hope – for Narcan, rescue, consent to treatment.
Narcan came. She began to breathe, sucked oxygen from the mask,
        emerged from her airless tomb,
opened her eyes like a morning glory and bloomed back into the world.
        Not at this moment, but soon after,

after she had breathed more air and the air breathed her, her hand
        reached for my forearm, afraid to hold on // afraid
to let go. And we had our conversation of eyes – her eyes told mine
        the craving would soon be coming back,
that her resuscitation was no remedy for the sorrow – my hope
        only a quick fix, not nearly enough.

Jockey Down

Meet the man, alone, sprawled on the grate, a gnarl on Baltimore's
    cold streetcorner.
His body nurses warmth from under the city. When steam rises
    from the grate,
I see him as he was before, son and brother in shining silks, rider up,
    winning the race at Pimlico.
Now his face is lost in rubble and urine, mired in a wet fog that lifts
    from pipes below,
as if it cared, to brush his hair in a whistling mist like the trill of some
    long-ago pretty bird who wears a feathered hat to the track.
The man lets go the horse's reins in his mind. His hand fumbles
    for the empty syringe spilled
to the street, leaking rider down, silks awry, head on a backpack saddle.

Bicycle mount tethered to cement, the street jockey turns his head
    to sing me a song of the unnatural, the unpoetic.
As the band begins to play in his head, his shoulders and hips spasm,
    gyrate.
He rides again on his street steed but cannot move from the grate.
    He hears little bells ring
like glasses clinking after a winning celebration or a wedding.
    He sees his pretty bird
hop on green grass in a churchyard. She stops, cocks her head
    to listen,
or to see into the underground as if she could have changed something.

His dance continues. The crowd roars as the pony stretches closer
    to the wire in a different race this time,
losing by only a nose, the length of a hypodermic needle, or a heartbeat,
    a distance almost inconsequential.
Steam rises in the pipes like ancient flutes playing. Wild bells ring.
    Multitudinous waters swirl beneath the streets,
keeping the pulseless beat as the band plays the song of jockey down.

The Widow Maker

The man in question was tall, standing well over six feet.
He had to reach down more than most to get to the level of snow.

One year he made it through much of winter, then March came,
dumped a foot of heavy white. The man in question kept his place

in the country immaculate. He came home from a long day's work
as snowfall ended and began shoveling, first the walkways

then the driveway: to get the car out if need be. He leaned
into the job, reached down farther than most, the angle

afforded him greater than most. After shoveling, shoveling,
shoveling, he became ill, stopped to rest and light a Lucky Strike.

The smoke encircled his perspiring dome like a blue halo. The man
in question felt no better. His wife thought he had a sudden case of the flu.

She and their teenage daughters drove him to the hospital, miles away
through the snow. The ER doctor ran an EKG and muttered:

tombstones! It's the widow maker all right, just as I suspected!
Horizontal now, on a flimsy gurney, the man in question

measured taller, still, than most, and his toes stood protuberantly blue
above the white sheets.

One-More-Day-Forever

for Hospice Care of Anne Arundel County, Maryland,
and Laura McClay

Pulling itself through dark's ring like silk,
snow surprised us before dawn came
calm and unburdened.

In that hour,
cold and still,
the night rose chose to bloom along the river.

Though no one would see it,
beauty was there,
a coming light felt just as it once glanced
off green-tree needles on the wild mountaintop.
A miracle it could find its way to pause,
grace our timber-hewn dwelling in the smoky valley:

empty now
except for the sleeve of snow, ice on a fir-tree bough
touching the rose in the image of the window,
and for the slender sound of wind,
light's footsteps descending the staircase,

as if the fragrance of the rose
and one-more-day-forever
would be coming down together.

Lake of Underwater Stones

Did you hear Frank Gabrin died
last night in NYC?

The lake – so still and close,
I count underwater stones on its shoreline.
Except for my counting, silence.

The virus?

Then a swan trumpets into wind above treetops
in sunrise far away:
a skein coming in to land on water.

Yes. He was the first ER doc in the country
to die of COVID-19.

A hundred feet up when I see them first,
bunched in cold spring air on the glidepath.

I'm stunned! Frank's charm,
quirky compassion – gone?

Wings bowed down. Tail feathers flared.
In slow flight with legs forward, straight out
like struts with webbed feet.

I know you two had a special bond. Didn't he
call you his Uncle Jonny?

All eleven splash water simultaneously:
a troupe of kite surfers safely touching down.

Yes, our mothers were Slovak.
Plus, I broke him in as a newbie.

The trumpeter swans are more natural
than people I know
with their digital devices, anxieties.
The swans create something unexpected:
a simple, meaningful perspective,

A tribute is airing tomorrow morning
on the 'Today' show.

something they didn't know they were giving:

Thanks, I'll look for
it

a revelation of peace,

and write Frank's story –
to circulate in the
department.

something otherwise unreachable

Our story.

I can keep inside me for a long time:

I'm at work now.
Text you again when I learn more.
Pray for a
remedy, a vaccine.

even as long as I live.

Frank's Story: Emergency Physician Who Fought COVID-19 Hand-to-Hand

We were in trenches together. The front line. The pit. Emergency Medicine. Busy place. Rough blue-collar town. Canton. HOF stabbings. Detroit cocaine connection. Dayton heroin. Parking lot fentanyl overdoses. Babies born in ambulances. Teenagers dead on prom night. Trauma, sepsis, meningitis, Corona-SARS, strokes, heart attacks. Helipad outside the glass door, bulletproof. Heart cath lab at the door, stent ready. Something you can never forget – though you might want to. Fighting for a common cause. Forming a permanent bond. You touch your brother's soul, clutch your sister's heart.

Frank Gabrin was a gifted clinician. Along with the usual traits that led to this distinction, he possessed some irregularities. Frank was an ER doc. ER docs tend to be more like regular people than other physicians, don't take the "doctor thing" so seriously, let it go to their heads. They're versatile. Frank had plenty of the regular in him. He could relate, even see things others didn't necessarily look for in people, such as eyeballing a jacket for a fray or a shoe for a muddy scuff to calculate what medicine might be afforded, possibly prescribing a less expensive drug that would work just as well.

He had a way about him people liked, could talk common talk, relate to you about a cooking class, art collection, kid's baseball game or clarinet lesson. He moved easy, liked to put his hand on your shoulder when explaining something, especially if it was sad, perhaps about your mother or daughter dying or another life event just as tragic. Frank could do everything well, effortlessly – things with his hands like suturing, rapid sequence intubation, reducing a dislocated hip, placing a chest tube or central I.V. line in a patient's neck.

But Frank had a problem, an irregularity. Sometimes he'd argue with people. Mostly it had nothing to do with medical diagnoses or treatment. Usually, it involved a subject some might consider stupid, like the kind of car a person drove if they bragged about it, or maybe a snide comment someone made about another person being fat or gay. Or maybe he'd get in a tiff with a consultant who didn't want to admit an uninsured garbage man to the hospital when he had pneumonia and a low oxygen level. Or maybe it was an all-out war with the hospital CEO or Medical Director about a comment he made to a family member he didn't know was on the hospital board – about how the fur coat his wife wore seemed a bit gaudy, or at 3 am, after examining the rash she had on her buttocks, noticed she was sporting expensive French underwear, then remarked about it.

Frank was a piece of work. He volunteered for the night shift. Sometimes, when a person works late into the night and it's really busy, he gets overly tired, almost drunk. Words can then come out of his mouth he might not ordinarily say. That was Frank. For this reason, he moved around from hospital to hospital, ended up in New York City. I worked with Frank for nearly 10 years, got to know him. Sometimes he thought he was invincible because he was a two-time cancer survivor. He was on replacement testosterone therapy, thinking perhaps the testosterone contributed to or was the sole cause of his odd, somewhat aggressive behavior toward some people who were basically jackasses to begin with. We talked about it once. His oncologist decreased his dose. For a while he seemed to get in less trouble.

I always felt Frank was right about most things, about his arguments, all the things he believed in, the ideals he was committed to. But, for sure, Frank was wrong about one thing: he was not invincible. Long before its peak in NYC, the virus got him. He died of COVID-19. Frank was a compassionate warrior. I loved him. His mother was Slovak just like mine. He called me his Uncle Jon. Frank was a damn good doctor and even better human being. I wish I could write him a letter or hug him, tell him how much I loved him. I wish I could put my hand on his shoulder now just the way he put his on mine once. I wish I could see his eyes sparkle, hear him laugh after telling me: *Uncle Jonny, you got an old soul, man! I can only imagine all the trouble it's seen, all the places it's been. Here, have another cabbage roll. It's halupki, Mother's recipe.*

Garden of Roses in Frost: For the Global Vaccine Poem Project

Dear Vaccine,

In our rose garden, we prayed

your radiance would suffuse the darkness,

prayed we might return

to the way we were.

Days longer, nights shorter.

Masks removed, not discarded.

In my mind, I took pictures of it all:

my two-year-old grandson, Joey, in his mask,

eyes bemused, the way they met mine.

Our connecting glances brought him

to sit beside me, our legs next to each other.

When we came close to touching,

I could feel him getting larger and me

smaller. Coming and going in time

as we were, a sadness arose,

like a garden of roses in frost

that persisted until the space between

our bodies pulled us in.

As the day lengthened and light slanted,

our shadows merged with the shadows of roses,

and for an instant we touched –

though by now uncertain

whose touch was whose,

which was which.

River of Blood

> *Wars, grim wars I see, and the Tiber foaming*
> *with streams of blood.*
> —Sibyl to Aeneas in Vrigil's *Aeneid*

> *He turned their rivers to blood, so that they could not drink*
> *from their streams.*
> —Psalm 78:44

I have stood at the headwaters of a river of blood, been in with the blood,
    waded in it, had it splashed in my hair, my eyes.
I've had it pool on the floor in front of me, slid in it, had it cover
    my hands, arms.

I've seen the shit hit the fan, been in the shit. I've witnessed the fan become
    a chainsaw,
severing a leg from a body brought to me in a plastic garbage bag
    on ice,
a tourniquet placed on the injured stump, a stranglehold to stop the bleeding.

I've paddled across a current of blood cascading off the side of a gurney,
    a waterfall of warm red
that smelled like sour death spewing from a bullet hole in a femoral artery.

Gravity was always the great director, funneled the pulsating stream of blood
    to a drain in the floor where it met
other connecting red streams from roll-over SUV's, penetrating chest traumas,
    drive-by shootings, drug deals gone bad.
With the addition of a dozen victims stabbed at random by a drug-crazed
    madman running through the crowd
at the NFL Hall of Fame festivities years ago, these streams collectively
    formed a raging river of blood.

I asked one of the contributors to my blood river: *where does all the blood*
    come from?
All he could say was he was minding his own business.

I think most of the blood from my river in Canton, Ohio,
springs from the Dayton-Detroit-Canton drug connection,
    then flows back to Mexico, Afghanistan and China,
a pipeline to great reservoirs of blood waiting
    to be processed, filtered, reissued.

One day I pledge to start a new river to wash away the one I've been struggling in.
    I'll call it the River of Sanguinity, the river
that flows with a yearning, an incessant clarity. Immaculate in its conception,
    I have trouble seeing this river now
for all the sticky red I'm in, for all the brown gunge in my eyes
    splattering off the fan that keeps on turning.

Take Me to the River

Place my ashes, please, into that small clay urn, the one
    Martha molded with her hands
on the wheel she turned in our farmhouse basement, the one
    fired in the kiln in the garage.
Then take me down to the Tuscarawas, to the bridge at Zoar
    below the old Inn on the River.

Walk with me on a sunny day, over the oak bridge-
    boards
to the center of the span, the spot where we watched
    the Kingfisher pair
feed their young in cottonwoods, where the river
    runs swiftest.
Drop a handful of me there – into wind – and witness
    my freefall – into current.
Watch the river do the rest . . . let me slip away.

Usher what's left of me to the path bordering Lone Willow
    Pond.
Escort me past the ash trees the beaver felled, past
    the fallen beech where I lingered
with the litter of spotted puppies romping in ferns
    along the feeder creek.
Walk me a little farther to the concavity in the field
    on the south-end hillside of our farm,
just beyond the Twin Oaks as they shoulder the evening sun.
    Adam knows the field and place I'm talking about.

The one where deer emerge from pines at half-light to browse
    on blackberry brambles beneath the red-apple tree.
A large whiterack beds there in the shallow indentation
    on starlit nights,
listens to wind in oaks on the conservancy ridge.

The field
where the wild turkey hen nested in the concavity one spring,
    shielding her poults under outstretched wings
during a downpour of cold rain. The field where I watched
    the white dragonfly
light on a multifloral rose bush. Martha painted her picture
    when I came back from mowing hay to tell her.

Place the urn in the ground there – into that soft depression
    in the long grass of the field –
not too deep. I want to be aware of the overall, the goings-on
    above me, hear the echoes of the Great Horned Owls calling.
Then cover the urn with a flat, round sandstone off the ridge
    above the squirrel woods where cattle lay in shade.
Leah knows these stones. Be certain it's not too thick:
    a couple inches of rock would do nicely.

This landing zone, at the stone, is where the white dragonfly
    will pause –
she resting above and me beneath – where I'll feel the vibrations
    of her wings
through the sedimentary layers of time as I slip away
    into the peace
of the good ground where Martha and I raised our family
    on the farm at Lone Willow.
The dragonfly, coming to the stone, will draw from that flame
    of life's fire beneath my bones.

A Sudden Sensation of Openness

I

As I wait here with my weaknesses and beliefs, sorted and assembled,
      the horizon's sky
at dusk changes from purple to orange. Something dark slips
      ahead of me,
moves from imaginable to unimaginable, and a sudden sensation
      of openness occurs.
Wind bends tall leaves of grass before the hill, lays them down
      flat to earth, the path clearly defined.

II

That evening in the Kansas sunset while walking a straight-line road
      that bisected fields of grain and grass
to the one hill in the distance, if I squinted, a mile-long herd of bison
      kicked up clouds of dry soil,
colored the horizon purple. When the skyline turned orange
      like prairie fire, I felt the urge to follow,
though in reality, the buffalo were gone, and the dust, like fire
      in the sky, was from tractors
plowing mile after mile of prairie. Still, dust in the wind
      on my face
felt like the ragged earth of buffalo. The land trembled
      with both new and old impermanence.

III

From above, in sunrise far away, throated notes of an oriole
      warble *the worst is over*
across the fields of purple amaranth and golden wheat. I find
      I will not be leaving today
        but go on as a presence
        in the overall of light:
     weightless, suspended, wind-drifting,
       anticipating at any moment
     a change into words everywhere.

Acknowledgments

The author wishes to thank the editors of journals and venues in which versions of these poems have appeared.

Evening Street Review: "A Soft Depression in Snow"

I Thought I Heard A Cardinal Sing: Ohio's Appalachian Voices Anthology 2022: "End of the Road;" "The Cardinal's Broken Song"

Global Vaccine Poem Project (Collaboration of Kent State University and the University of Arizona): Aired on *NPR* April 16, 2021: "Garden of Roses in Frost"

Common Threads: Ohio Poetry Association Annual Journal of Work 2021: "Springhouse"

Common Threads: Ohio Poetry Association Annual Journal of Work 2023: "Diminutive Bird" (under title of "In the Oldest Mountains": 2nd Place Winner Ohio Eco-Poetry Contest)

Open Earth Foundation's Open Earth III 2023: "Diminutive Bird" (under title of "In the Oldest Mountains")

Cuyahoga County Public Library Weblog: Read & Write: 30 Days of Poetry, April 2022: "She Bloomed Back into the World"

Edith Chase Symposium Anthology 2018: "Morning-After Campfire"

Resurrection River Poems: 2019 Edith Chase Symposium Anthology: "Beauty in the Echo of the Crooked River"

Under The Blossum That Hangs On The Bough: 2020 Edith Chase Symposium Anthology: "Applewood, Butterflies and Summer Rain"

The Sky Was Always Underground: A Lyric Memoir of Appalachia (Sunbury Press 2023): "Sitting in the Same Dark;" "This Light of Home;" "Springhouse;" "End of the Road;" "Applewood, Butterflies and Summer Rain;" "Rolling on Red Dog;" "The Widow Maker"

Gratitude to the two influential poets I found my way to know: James Dickey, who instructed me formally at the University of South Carolina, and Maj Ragain, of Kent State University, who taught me informally with the exchange of poems and letters.

Thanks to Jamie DeMonte, Gregory Vasse, Mary Greer, Annie Dawid, Carol D Guerrero-Murphy, and Lee Elliott for their help with the manuscript.

And thanks to the team at Cornerstone Press, especially director Dr. Ross Tangedal, editor Maria Scherer, cover designer Carolyn Czerwinski, media director Zoie Dinehart, and the entire editorial and production staffs.

JONATHAN GRAHAM was born along the Ohio River in Martins Ferry, breathed air that chugged from smokestacks at Wheeling Steel, and grew up not far from there in an ethnic enclave of immigrant Slovak coal miners. Drafted into the military and serving first as a medic, then later in aviation, he went on to study poetry as a graduate student of American Literature/Creative Writing and medicine, becoming an Emergency Physician. Jon resides on a farm/sanctuary near the village of Zoar in the hilly woodlands of East Central Ohio.